My Christmas Tree
and Other Poems of the Season

Compiled and illustrated by Ann Schweninger

A GOLDEN BOOK • NEW YORK
Western Publishing Company, Inc., Racine, Wisconsin 53404

In the Week When Christmas Comes

This is the week when Christmas comes.

Let every pudding burst with plums,
And every tree bear dolls and drums,
 In the week when Christmas comes.

Let every hall have boughs of green,
With berries glowing in between,
 In the week when Christmas comes.

Let every doorstep have a song,
Sounding the dark street along,
 In the week when Christmas comes.

Let every steeple ring a bell
With a joyful tale to tell,
 In the week when Christmas comes.

Let every night put forth a star
To show us where the heavens are,
 In the week when Christmas comes.

This is the week when Christmas comes.
 —*ELEANOR FARJEON*

At Christmas Time

In every house on every street
around and up and down
there's something special going on,
in every house in town:

Gifts to make
and lights to string
and sweets to bake
and bells to ring
(with snowflakes sifting down),
and shiny eyes
and dancy feet
in every house on every street,
on every street in town.

—AILEEN FISHER

Bundles

A bundle is a funny thing,
It always sets me wondering:
For whether it is thin or wide
You never know just what's inside.

Especially in Christmas week
Temptation is so great to peek!
Now wouldn't it be much more fun
If shoppers carried things undone?

—*JOHN FARRAR*

Christmas Tree

I'll find me a spruce
in the cold white wood
with wide green boughs
and a snowy hood.

I'll pin on a star
with five gold spurs
to mark my spruce
from the pines and firs.

I'll make me a score
of suet balls
to tie to my spruce
when the cold dusk falls,

And I'll hear next day
from the sheltering trees,
the Christmas carols
of the chickadees.

—*AILEEN FISHER*

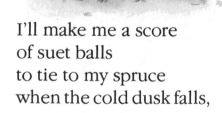

My Christmas Tree

Shine, Christmas Tree, shine!
Shine, shine, shine!
You are mine.
With your tinselly strands
And your shimmering bands;
With your glittering star,
You are mine, Christmas Tree,
You are.

Shine, Christmas Tree, shine!
Shine, shine, shine!
You are mine.
With your snowy popcorn,
Colored balls, silver horn;
With your lights all aglow,
You are mine, Christmas Tree,
I know.

—JAMES S. TIPPETT

from **Villagers All**

Villagers all, this frosty tide,
Let your doors swing open wide,
Though wind may follow, and snow beside,
Yet draw us in by your fire to bide.
 Joy shall be yours in the morning!

 —*KENNETH GRAHAME*

Day Before Christmas

We have been helping with the cake
　　And licking out the pan,
And wrapping up our packages
　　As neatly as we can.
And we have hung our stockings up
　　Beside the open grate,
And now there's nothing more to do
　　　　Except
　　　　　　To
　　　　　　　　Wait!

—*MARCHETTE CHUTE*

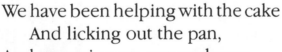

Stocking Song on Christmas Eve

Welcome, Christmas! heel and toe,
Here we wait thee in a row.
Come, good Santa Claus, we beg—
Fill us tightly, foot and leg.

Fill us quickly ere you go—
Fill us till we overflow.
That's the way! and leave us more
Heaped in piles upon the floor.

Little feet that ran all day
Twitch in dreams of merry play;
Little feet that jumped at will
Lie all pink, and warm, and still.

See us, how we lightly swing;
Hear us, how we try to sing.
Welcome, Christmas! heel and toe,
Come and fill us ere you go.

Here we hang till some one nimbly
Jumps with treasure down the chimney.
Bless us! how he'll tickle us!
Funny old St. Nicholas!

—*MARY MAPES DODGE*

Christmas Eve

On a winter night
When the moon is low
The rabbits hop on the frozen snow.
The woodpecker sleeps in his hole in the tree
And fast asleep is the chickadee.

Twelve o'clock
And the world is still
As the Christmas star comes over the hill.
The angels sing, and sing again:
"Peace on earth, goodwill to men."

—*MARION EDEY*

A Christmas Carol

Everywhere, everywhere Christmas to-night!
Christmas in lands of the fir-tree and pine,
Christmas in lands of palm tree and vine,
Christmas, where snow peaks stand solemn and white,
Christmas where cornfields lie sunny and bright!
Everywhere, everywhere Christmas to-night!

—PHILLIPS BROOKS

Long, Long Ago

Winds thru the olive trees
  Softly did blow,
Round little Bethlehem,
  Long, long ago.

Sheep on the hillside lay
  Whiter than snow,
Shepherds were watching them,
  Long, long ago.

Then from the happy sky,
  Angels bent low,
Singing their songs of joy,
  Long, long ago.

For in a manger bed,
  Cradled we know,
Christ came to Bethlehem,
  Long, long ago.

Christmas Song

Why do the bells of Christmas ring?
Why do little children sing?

Once a lovely shining star,
Seen by shepherds from afar,
Gently moved until its light
Made a manger's cradle bright.

There a darling baby lay,
Pillowed soft upon the hay,
And its mother sung and smiled:
"This is Christ, the Holy Child."

Therefore bells for Christmas ring,
Therefore little children sing.

—*EUGENE FIELD*

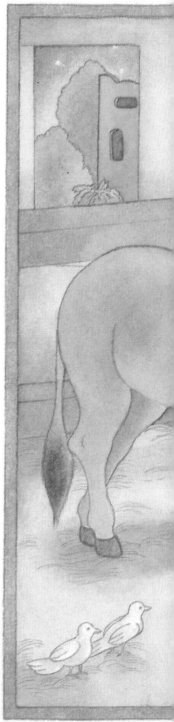

Christmas Bells

I heard the bells on Christmas Day
Their old, familiar carols play,
    And wild and sweet
    The words repeat
Of peace on earth, goodwill to men!
      —*HENRY WADSWORTH LONGFELLOW*

Away in a Manger

Away in a manger, no crib for His bed,
The little Lord Jesus laid down His sweet head.
The stars in the sky looked down where He lay,
The little Lord Jesus, asleep on the hay.

from **Christmas Morning**

On Christmas day, when fires were lit,
And all our breakfasts done,
We spread our toys out on the floor
And played there in the sun.

—*KATHARINE PYLE*

Sing We All Merrily

Sing we all merrily
    Christmas is here,
The day we love best
    Of all days in the year.

Bring forth the holly,
    The box and the bay,
Deck out our cottage
    For glad Christmas day.

We all sing merrily,
    Draw near the fire,
Sister and brother,
    Grandson and sire.

Now Christmas Is Come

Now Christmas is come
    Let's beat up the drum,
And call all our neighbors together,
    And when they appear,
Let's make them such cheer
    As will keep out the wind and the weather.

—*WASHINGTON IRVING*

Merry Christmas

God bless the master of this house,
    The mistress bless also,
And all the little children
    That round the table go;
And all our kin and kinsmen,
    That dwell both far and near,
I wish you a merry Christmas,
    And a happy New Year.

Acknowledgments

Grateful acknowledgment is made to the following publishers, authors, and other copyright holders for permission to reprint copyrighted materials. While all reasonable efforts have been made to find the holders of copyrighted materials, any omissions or errors will be corrected in future editions, and copyrights properly acknowledged.

Marchette Chute for "Day Before Christmas," from *Rhymes About the Country,* copyright © 1941, renewed © 1969.

Harper & Row, Inc., for "In the Week When Christmas Comes," from *Eleanor Farjeon's Poems for Children,* copyright © 1927 by Eleanor Farjeon, renewed © 1953. "At Christmas Time," from *In One Door and out the Other: A Book of Poems* by Aileen Fisher, copyright © 1964 by The Instructor Publications, Inc. "My Christmas Tree," from *Crickety Cricket! The Best-Loved Poems of James S. Tippett,* copyright © 1973 by Martha K. Tippett.

Plays, Inc., for "Christmas Tree," from *Christmas Plays and Programs,* copyright © 1960, 1970 by Aileen Fisher.

Charles Scribner's Sons for "Christmas Eve," from *Open the Door,* copyright © 1949 by Marion Edey and Dorothy Grider.

Yale University Press for "Bundles," from *Songs for Parents,* copyright © 1921 by John Farrar.